I CAN BE A
BIOLOGIST

By Paul P. Sipiera

Prepared under the direction of Robert Hillerich, Ph.D.

CP CHILDRENS PRESS®
CHICAGO

Library of Congress Cataloging-in-Publication Data

Sipiera, Paul, P.
  I can be a biologist / by Paul Sipiera.
      p.   cm.
  Summary: Describes the training required to be a
biologist and the different kinds of jobs available in the
field.
  ISBN 0-516-01966-X
  1. Biology—Vocational guidance—Juvenile
literature.   2.   Biologists—Juvenile literature.
[1.   Biology—Vocational guidance.   2.   Occupations.
3.   Vocational guidance.]   I.   Title.
QH314.S57   1992
574'.023—dc20   91-39243
                                                       CIP
                                                       AC

95-631 ✓

Dedicated to the memory of Patrick,
Paul, and Kathleen Leonard.

farmer

biologist

medicine

space medicine

food plants

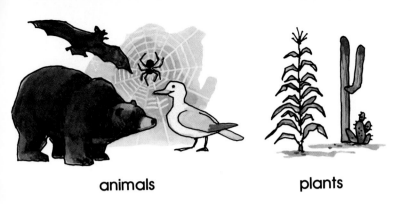

animals

plants

living things

minerals

non-living things

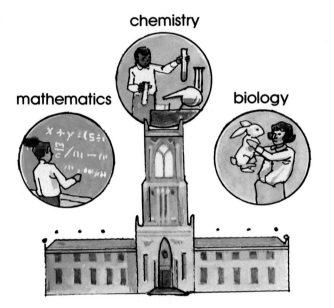

chemistry

mathematics

biology

university

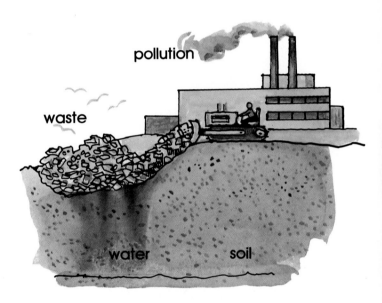

pollution

waste

water

soil

environment

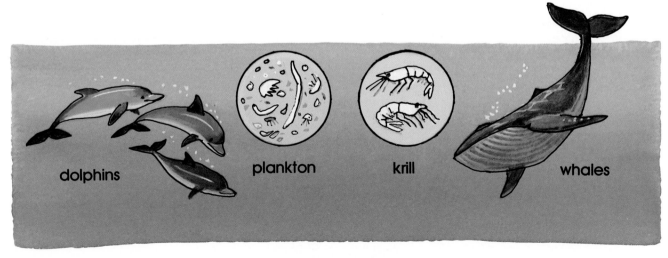

dolphins

plankton

krill

whales

marine biology

Red-eyed vireo feeds its young (above left).
Different kinds of rock (above right) make up the Earth.
Grass and flowers are just two of the many kinds of plants (below).

animals

plants

living things

When you go outdoors, look around you carefully. Do you see birds in the trees and flowers in the ground? Do you see any rocks?

Do you know which ones are living things? Birds are animals, and trees are plants. They are alive. Rocks are made of minerals. They were never alive.

minerals

non-living things

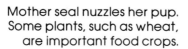

Mother seal nuzzles her pup.
Some plants, such as wheat,
are important food crops.

Rocks cannot breathe,
eat, or reproduce. Living
things—animals and
plants—do all these things.

Biology is the science
that describes living
things. People who study
biology are called

biologists. Knowing about
biology helps us understand
our world better.

Who can become a
biologist? Almost anyone
can—if they have an
interest in science. Have

biologist

Student
examines
a biology
experiment.

Spider (left) weaving its web.
Student (above) studies the many
different types of cactus plants.

you ever wondered how
a spider weaves its web?
Or how a cactus can
survive without rain? If
you have, then you may
be a biologist someday.

8

Becoming a biologist takes many years of study. You must go to a university to study mathematics and chemistry, as well as biology. It is hard work, but it can be fun, too!

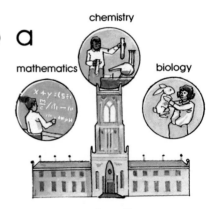

chemistry

mathematics

biology

university

Students (left) learn about biology by studying models of animals. Some students (right) perform experiments in the laboratory.

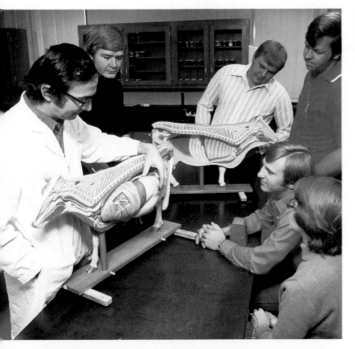

medicine

farmer

Where do biologists work? Some work in medicine. Others help protect our environment. Many biologists work with farmers to improve our food supply.

Microbiologists (left) prepare samples for medical research.

Biologists (below) help farmers grow better crops.

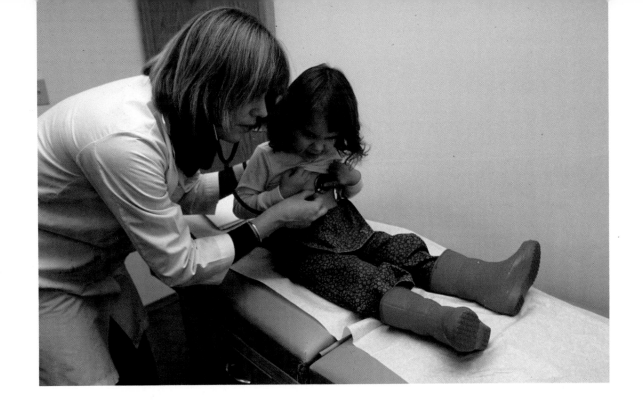

A person who wants to become a doctor or nurse must study biology. Dentists also must know biology. They all have to learn how the human body is put together and how it works.

11

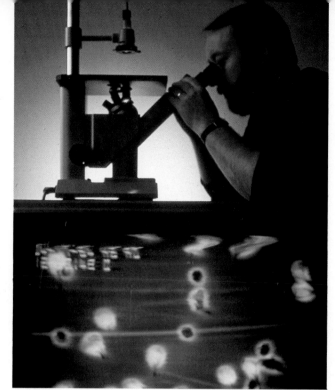

Special microscopes help the biologist learn more about cells and how they work.

Some biologists study cells. They learn how cells form, reproduce, and eventually die. Others study the causes of diseases. Once the cause of a disease is found, scientists can look for a cure.

12

Biologists help doctors learn about diseases and how to cure them.

Biologists also work in laboratories. They test blood and tissue samples. They help doctors find out why people are sick. Space medicine is an important part of biology.

space medicine

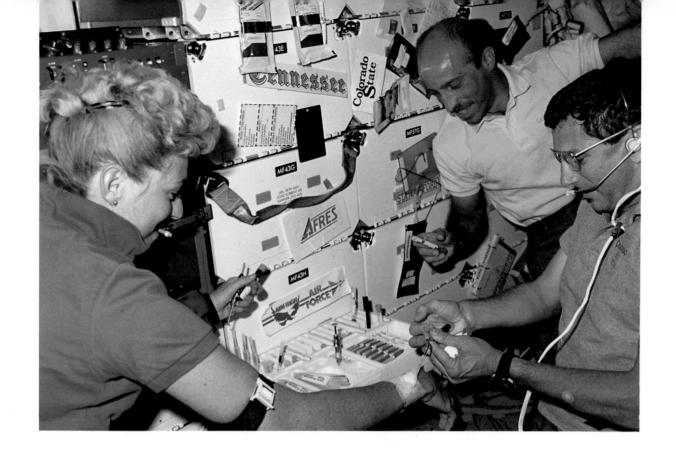

Space medicine is
helping us to
learn how to live
outside the Earth.

Experiments conducted
on board the Space Shuttle
have studied the effects
of space travel on humans.
Other space studies have
tested new ways to
make better medicines.

medicine

14

Some biologists (left) work with farm animals.
Biologist (right) looks at tissues from disease-free
strawberry plants.

Some biologists work
with animals. They learn
about our pets, farm
animals, and wildlife.

Other biologists develop
new kinds of food plants
that can resist diseases.

food plants

Using helpful
insects to eat
harmful ones
keeps our
environment
clean of
poisons.

They have learned how to use certain insects to protect crops. This means that farmers do not need to use poisonous chemicals to get rid of the harmful insects. And this helps keep our environment clean.

Biologists help solve
environmental problems.
They collect samples of
polluted water and soil.
They find out what
caused the pollution, and

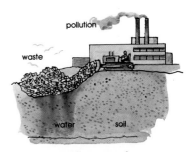

environment

Biologists (left) study polluted waters to help clean up our planet. Some biologists (below) study soils in order to learn what types of crops would grow best in them.

17

Oil spills are very harmful to many different kinds of life.

they suggest ways to clean it up.

When an oil spill occurs at sea, biologists study its effect on animals, plants, and people.

Studying the environment is a very important job for the biologist.

Biologists work with city planners. Cities need to set aside space for parks and wetland. Biologists help decide which sites should be preserved as open space.

Where to put our waste is becoming an important question.

Waste management is another problem studied by biologists. Where do you put a garbage dump? How will it affect the surrounding communities? How long does it take garbage to decompose? Biologists can answer questions like these.

Biologists sometimes use graphs and charts to organize information they collect.

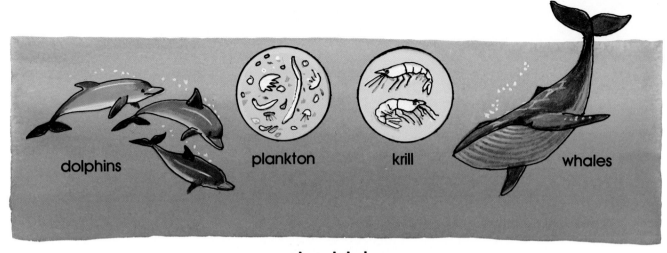

marine biology

Marine biologists study the wonderful forms of life that live in the sea. Their subjects range from whales and dolphins to small life forms, such as krill and plankton. We need to understand the place each living thing has in the food chain.

Biologists study whales to learn their habits.

Scientist examines a starfish.

Dolphins are mammals like whales and people.

Proper use of the sea's resources will benefit all the people.

Perhaps the most important job of the marine biologist is to protect sea life from humans. Overfishing and hunting threaten many species with extinction.

When accidents happen, the biologist is there
to advise workers on the best way to clean up the spill.

Oil and chemical spills
kill millions of animals.
Biologists make people
aware of the harm they
do and how their actions
affect our planet.

Park naturalists keep the plants and animals under their care healthy.

Biologists also work as naturalists in state or national parks. They help protect the park environment. They teach

National parks are wonderful places
to study biology.

people about nature. A
summer job in a national
park is a good way for a
biology student to gain
valuable experience.

Scientist (above) examines a wheat plant looking for wheat-scab disease.

Students (left) learn much about biology in school laboratories.

The study of biology offers many ways to learn about living things. It helps us protect life on Earth. As a biologist, you

28

Learning about biology can be exciting.

might discover life on Mars or a cure for the common cold. Who knows? It's up to you to find out!

WORDS YOU SHOULD KNOW

biology(by•AHL•uh•gee)—the study of living things

cell(SELL)—the very small basic unit of living material usually having a wall or membrane around it

chemicals(KEM•ih•kilz)—substances that make up the world's materials. Chemicals are often harmful to living things

chemistry(KEM•iss•tree)—the science that studies what substances are made of, how they combine with other substances, and how they behave under certain conditions

decompose(dee•kum•POZE)—to decay; to break down into its parts

environment(en•VYE•run•mint)—the things that surround a plant or an animal; the lands and waters of the earth

extinction(ex•TINK•shun)—the dying out of a species of plant or animal

food chain(FOOD CHAYNE)—a relationship among organisms in which each feeds on a plant or an animal below it in the chain and is then eaten by an animal above it

inhabit(in•HAB•it)—to occupy; to live on or in

krill(KRILL)—tiny shrimplike animals that live in the ocean

laboratory(LAB • ra • tor • ee) —a place where a scientist works

marine biologist(muh • REEN by • AHL • uh • gist) —a person who studies the animals and plants that live in the ocean

mineral(MIN • ril) —substances such as iron, rocks, or coal that are found in the ground

naturalist(NATCH • rih • list) —a person who studies nature, especially one who works outdoors

plankton(PLANK • tun) —tiny plants and animals that live in the ocean

pollution(puh • LOO • shun) —the dirtying of the earth's air, water, and land

reproduce(ree • pro • DOOCE) —to produce young; to give birth or lay eggs

space medicine(SPAYSS MEH • di • sin) —the study of the effects of space travel on the human body

tissue(TISH • oo) —a material made up of cells; part of a plant or animal, such as muscle tissue

university(yoo • nih • VER • sih • tee) —a college or other school of higher learning

wetlands(WET • landz) —lands that are covered with shallow water; swamps; marshes

INDEX

PHOTO CREDITS

About the Author

Paul P. Sipiera is a professor of earth sciences at William Rainey Harper College in Palatine, Illinois. His principal research interests are in the study of meteorites and volcanic rocks. He has participated in the United States Antarctic Research Program and is a member of The Explorers Club. He is currently serving as president of the Planetary Studies Foundation. When he is not studying science, he can be found traveling the world or working on his farm in Galena, Illinois.